Praise for *Mixing I*

MW00978584

Zeik Saidman demonstrates i
for the less privileged, and his g
make an enormous difference. He brings passion, enthusiasm, and a
sense of optimism to his work of making our country a much better
place.

> *Federico Peña, Senior Advisor to Vestar Capital, former Mayor of*
> *Denver, U.S. Secretary of Transportation, U.S. Secretary of Energy*

Anyone interested in community or labor organizing should check
this book out. I worked with Zeik Saidman and learned a lot from doing so. I also learned a lot about organizing giving this a read. So if you
are wondering whether to become an organizer or whether to become
an organizer again give this a read and I bet you decide to do it.

> *Richard Bensinger, Director of Organizing for*
> *United Auto Workers (UAW) and founder and former Director*
> *of the Organizing Institute of the AFL-CIO*

Zeik Saidman has great stories, but more importantly he lifts up the
public skills that are the thread through them all. Saidman is one of the
best, and we can all learn from him.

> *Mary Helgeson Keefe, Executive Director of Hope Communities*
> *in Minneapolis and former community organizer*
> *with the Industrial Areas Foundation*

Zeik Saidman's community organizing skills were essential to his success as a project consultant and facilitator for The Colorado Trust.
He exhibited an incredible ability to lead communities through challenging issues by helping stakeholders understand the importance of
strong relationships as well as the need to work together to address
potentially divisive community problems. Saidman's leadership was
instrumental in helping The Trust achieve its goal of creating community to solve challenging problems.

> *Carol Breslau, Vice President for National Services & Community*
> *Impact for Mercy Housing and former Vice President*
> *of Programs at the Colorado Trust*

★★★★ *THE SKILLS OF ORGANIZING* ★★★★

MIXING IT UP
IN THE PUBLIC ARENA

*A career as a community organizer, union organizer,
political aide, and public facilitator*

A. Zeik Saidman

PUBLICATIONS

MIXING IT UP IN THE PUBLIC ARENA
A career as a community organizer, union organizer,
political aide, and public facilitator
by A. Zeik Saidman

Edited by Gregory F. Augustine Pierce
Cover and text design and typesetting by Patricia A. Lynch

Published by ACTA Publications, 4848 N. Clark Street, Chicago, IL
60640, (800) 397-2282, www.actapublications.com

ISBN: 978-0-87946-514-8
Printed in the United States of America by Total Printing Systems
Year 20 19 18 17 16 15 14 13
Printing 10 9 8 7 6 5 4 3 2 First

♻Text printed on 30% post-consumer recycled paper.

CONTENTS

★★★★

A NOTE FROM THE PUBLISHER

★★★★

I first met Zeik Saidman on January 2, 1970, on the steps of the Industrial Areas Foundation (IAF) Training Institute at 528 N. Michigan Avenue next to the Boul Mich tavern, at which we spent many evenings over the next few months. We had both been hired by the Student National Education Association to train to go onto college campuses and "get something orga nized" as Ed Chambers, the executive director of the IAF would say. This was, literally, only months before Kent State.

Zeik had already worked for a couple of years in El Paso as a VISTA volunteer, so at least he had some idea what being an organizer was, but I was just out of a Catholic seminary and was totally intimidated by the entire organizing culture, which was, from what I could see, based on bravado, booze, and machismo and worshipped at the shrine of Saul Alinsky, who was still alive but not very active by that time.

But the IAF was also the only group I could find who cared as much as I did about finding some way to create real change in our country after the tumultuous protests of the sixties, and people like Ed Chambers and Dick Harmon and Peter Martinez were willing to train young people like Zeik and me in the basic skills of organizing. So we hung around and learned, mostly by osmosis or by trial and error.

There were tons of interesting people hanging

around the IAF in those days. Many of them burned themselves out and left organizing, others (especially the women) got angry with the IAF staff and went out and formed their own groups, and some of us stuck around.

Zeik and I became great friends and have remained so all our lives. We both worked for IAF projects throughout the 1970s and into the 1980s, when we both transitioned into other careers. Zeik went into union organizing in Denver and eventually worked for Mayor Federico Peña. I eventually ended up as a publisher in Chicago, where I specialize in books on religion, baseball, and community organizing—the three things I actually know enough about to publish books on them.

Both Zeik and I stayed involved in our communities in a variety of ways, and now, over 40 years since we met on the steps of the IAF headquarters, we are at the point in our lives when we have both the desire and the perspective to reflect on what he calls "mixing it up in the public arena." I had already started publishing a series of booklets on community organizing by people like Ed Chambers, Mike Gecan, and Ernesto Cortes, so when Zeik brought me a whitepaper that he had done for his last job as a facilitator/project consultant at the University of Colorado Denver, I thought it would make an excellent addition to the series.

There are two dueling quotes in the organizing arena that I have heard all my life. The first I have seen attributed to both Dorothy Day and Mother Teresa, and it goes like this: "We are called to be faithful, not effective." The other I'm pretty sure was said by Vince Lombardi, the iconic coach of the Green Bay Packers: "Winning isn't everything; it's the only thing."

I believe most people who mix it up in the public arena for a lifetime as Zeik and I have done come to realize neither quote is quite accurate and the truth lies somewhere in between. Yes, we are supposed to be effective in our activism, as Vince Lombardi insisted, because too many people are counting on us to be satisfied with only our good intentions. Being faithful, as Dorothy Day and Mother Teresa seemed to advocate, is not good enough. And yet, anyone who understands public life knows that we will lose a fair share of our fights. Otherwise we simply are not fighting for enough. And so we must also be faithful, even if we are not always effective.

That, in a nutshell, is the story that Zeik Saidman tells here. His career in the public arena has been both faithful and effective, even though he has had his share of failure, disappointment, and loss. And so will anyone who tries to make the world a little better place than they find it.

Gregory F. Augustine Pierce
President and Co-Publisher
ACTA Publications

INTRODUCTION

★★★★

In the midst of a busy career, few of us have the luxury of time to think about what makes us get up every morning and why we do what we do. Only later, reflecting on forty-five years in the trenches as a community organizer in a variety of capacities, did I arrive at the realization that I was driven all along by my idealism and the cultural milieu in which my generation came of age believing that we really could change the world.

One of the lessons drilled into to me at the Industrial Areas Foundation (IAF) was an understanding of the tension that exists between "the world as it is" and "the world as you would like it to be." This lesson has been incorporated into speeches by both Barack and Michelle Obama. Idealism tempered by the political reality of knowing when you can win is the art of successful work in the public arena and was a continuing theme over my career.

I was drawn to be an advocate for the disadvantaged and the underdogs of our society, whether I was working as a community organizer, union organizer or even as a mayoral aide. Perhaps this commitment was shaped by my childhood experiences when we were the only Jewish family in a small town in rural Pennsylvania and I learned to readily identify with the feeling of being the outsider. I also read Holocaust literature growing up, and the dismay and rage I felt about what the Nazis did to those who they considered inferior peoples (gays, Slavs, Gypsies, Jews) gave me the cold anger and determination to fight for the have-nots.

The fights were never easy and we didn't win them all, but in thinking about what kept me going from the time I was an innocent man in his early twenties until I had become a worldly old hand in his mid-sixties, I have to admit a big part was the excitement of political battle.

The grassroots organizations I was involved with ran actions against powerful institutions and formidable public figures. Our leaders were on TV. Issues we championed were in the media. When we would win on a demand, I felt I truly was changing the world.

The work was never boring. There was a limited shelf life for the issues, so it was intellectually stimulating to immerse myself in something important, mobilize local leaders to confront the problem, and then move on to the next challenge. Furthermore, principles that were important to me such as fairness, equity, equality, and justice were the focus of our efforts. I never felt that I was compromising my ideals.

Along the way, I forged deep public relationships with many everyday folks. I also particularly enjoyed the ethics, humor, and intellect of the clergy from the different faith traditions that I met when building congregational-based citizen organizations. At the same time, my work was aligned with my own faith tradition. The concept of *Tikkun Olam*—healing of the world—is a central tenet of Judaism. The Talmud teaches "to save one life is to save the world." I felt my work resonated with those tenets of faith.

Finally, though I focused on my own education and development early on, as I matured personally and professionally I discovered real satisfaction in seeing everyday people grow and develop as leaders. Often, years after we had worked together, I would learn that I had changed ordinary people's lives in ways I never realized.

When I contemplate the future after retiring from my job at the School of Public Affairs at the University of Colorado Denver, a Yiddish saying comes to mind: "Man plans, G-d laughs." With any luck, my partner and wife of over 40 years, Alana Smart, and I will continue to lead relevant lives and remain in good health. I know with our shared values we will find ways to be involved in public issues for many years to come.

My hope is that you enjoy my reflections and gain some new insights from a regular guy who mixed it up in the public arena for a long, long time.

EL PASO, TEXAS

1967 to 1969
Volunteers in Service to America (VISTA)

★★★★

I was a newly-minted 20-year-old college graduate in 1967 when I boarded a plane to El Paso. I remember lifting off and seeing those familiar small, green mountains and continuous little towns along the mighty Susquehanna River of northeast Pennsylvania where I grew up. A few years before I graduated, President Kennedy had fired up young people with his now famous quote, "Ask not what your country can do for you—ask what you can do for your country." President Johnson had declared the War on Poverty. I was idealistic and so I joined VISTA. My placement was to the west Texas city of El Paso, right across the border from Juarez, Mexico. What a change in both the physical and cultural environment it was for me! El Paso is in the desert, surrounded by barren mountains and almost always baking under a blazing sun. Northeast Pennsylvania is bathed in rain and features many gray days when the clouds hang low in the sky.

The cultural change was just as profound. I had never met a Mexican-American till I arrived in El Paso. My VISTA group was the first ever sent to there. Among the VISTA volunteers were Hispanics from across the Southwest. This was a time of activism. The zeitgeist of that era was characterized by charismatic leaders speaking out and acting boldly on social issues. Cesar Chavez, Reies Tijerina, Corky Gonzales, and members of organizations such as the Brown Berets all were making their presence felt. And of course, the Vietnam War played out on the evening news. Ironically, one of the major departure points for young soldiers to Vietnam was adjacent to El Paso. On the weekends we would see the soldiers from Fort Bliss partying in Juarez before they were shipped out. My VISTA colleagues thought it was a stupid and senseless war. In 1968, in the middle of my VISTA tour, the Rev. Martin Luther King, Jr., and Sen. Robert Kennedy were assassinated. Out of the sheer frustration of the insanity of it all, the VISTA volunteers stationed in the area marched around El Paso's main square carrying signs expressing their outrage.

One of my strongest memories of El Paso was the action taken against slum landlords. I was assigned to the Segundo Barrio (Second Ward). One of the boundaries of the neighborhood was a barbed wire fence along the Rio Grande; on the other side loomed Mexico. Many of the people in the Segundo Barrio lived in tenements called presidios. Several of these presidios had only outhouses for their residents. The organization that was fighting for the tenants was called Project MACHOS (Mexican-American Committee on Honor Opportunity and Service). The organizer behind the scene was a wealthy, left of center, Catholic Oklahoman named Tom Sinclair. Tom had read Saul Alinsky's books and was clever about thinking up tactics to use against people in power.

We transported the tenants in yellow school buses to the mesa where a few of their affluent land-lords—some of them of Hispanic ancestry—lived. We held prayer vigils in front of their magnificent homes. Older women covered their heads with shawls and knelt on the ground saying the rosary. The media featured stories about the action, which pushed the landlords to begin meeting with us and negotiating improvements in the tenements. Years later, almost all the buildings were torn down and decent public housing units were built.

REFLECTIONS

I learned that the powerless can have an impact when they organize. Congregations are networks of people with faith-based values. If it is a newsworthy story with human elements, the media will usually cover it. The media can be important allies in making a strong case to the public.

YELLOW SPRINGS, OHIO,
AND PUTNEY, VERMONT

Summer of 1969 to summer 1970
Graduate student in Master of Arts in Teaching
program at Antioch-Putney Graduate School

★★★★

Like many young people finishing a tour with VISTA,
I was trying to figure out where to channel my idealism. Teaching seemed like a good place. I had been
accepted in the Master of Arts in Teaching program
at Antioch College. I felt so much more worldly-
wise than the students I met that summer in Yellow
Springs. Traveling to Vermont with my student friend
Barbara Bash, we decided to bypass a music festival on
our route. The weather had been rainy and we didn't
know anything about this place called Woodstock.

While the music festival turned out to be historic,
the graduate program had very few placements avail-
able in public school districts. They did have an open-
ing at the Brattleboro Retreat, a mental institution,
however, so I decided that since I had a B.A. in psy-
chology, it could be a worthwhile experience while I
mulled a career path. Ultimately, it wasn't a very good
encounter, but at that age it was valuable to know that
I didn't want to pursue that kind of work.

Before I completed the program at Antioch, I was
invited to become a trainee at the Industrial Areas
Foundation (IAF) in Chicago. I negotiated an agree-

ment with the teaching program to use my experience in community organizing to earn the credits necessary to fulfill the coursework.

REFLECTIONS

Destiny sometimes intervenes and a different direction emerges. One of my favorite poems has always been Robert Frost's "The Road Not Taken." Also, at this point in my life, I was enamored by the world of community organizing. It seemed to be the kind of work that would try to harness the turmoil in our society and give voice to the powerless.

CHICAGO, ILLINOIS

1969 to 1975
Industrial Areas Foundation (IAF)

★ ★ ★ ★

When I arrived in the Windy City in December 1969, Judge Julius Hoffman was presiding over the circus known as the "Chicago Seven" trial. I was awed by the skyscrapers and the energy of the city that Carl Sandburg called the "hog butcher for the world." The IAF was founded by Saul Alinsky, the fountainhead of all community organizing. Saul was in his late sixties when I came to Chicago. I first heard him speak in a small room to would-be community organizers. I was impressed by his depth and remember he seemed low-key and old, since I was a brash 23-year-old. Saul didn't come across as the radical, rabble-rouser portrayed by the media. His demeanor seemed more that of a philosopher.

Over the next five years I worked in various projects out of Chicago with the support of the IAF. The most memorable were helping to create the Campaign Against Pollution (CAP) and acting as an advisor to the Menominee Native Americans' DRUMS organization.

CAP came into existence because the air on the South Side of Chicago was so polluted with emissions from the Commonwealth Edison power plants that it rained sulfuric acid. Paint on the cars parked in these neighborhoods faded. The IAF lead organizer, Pete

Martinez, supervised a cadre of young organizers in a grassroots fight against Com Ed. Using the Catholic parishes as a base of power, we focused on the company's annual stockholder meeting. My assignment was to recruit sympathetic students from local colleges and universities to attend. We billed it as the People's Stockholders meeting. It was an era of guerilla theater, and Studs Terkel, a writer and nationally known radio host, agreed to be the master of ceremonies for our meeting. We had a group of older women from one of the ladies parish societies perform the can-can. We collected stock proxies and tried to get our allies inside Com Ed's stockholders meeting. CAP turned out a couple thousand supporters to their meeting. Keeping the pressure on after this event, Mayor Richard Daley (the original) told representatives from Com Ed to meet with CAP. Daley didn't like this kind of antics in his city. It was the beginning of cleaning up the power plants.

The Menominee reservation was in far northeastern Wisconsin, but a large number of the Menominees lived in Chicago's Uptown area. I was hired by a foundation to be an advisor to DRUMS (Determination of Rights and Unity for Menominee Stockholders), an organization formed by activist members of the tribe. It was led by the charismatic Jim White. (His Native American name was Washinawatok.) The Bureau of Indian Affairs had decided that the Menominees were a successful tribe, in part because they were running a profitable lumber mill. The reservation's land had been divided and each member of the tribe had been given shares that were held by the First Wisconsin Trust Company, a large local bank. Unscrupulous realtors and their cohorts tried to get vulnerable (impoverished and often alcoholic) members of the tribe to sign over their stocks to them. Real estate interests wanted the stock options so they could get title to the land and build vacation homes along the Wolf River. One of the Alinsky-style tactics we employed targeted the First Wisconsin's flagship bank in Milwaukee. We had members of the tribe open savings accounts with pennies, disrupting the bank's business. As part of that action, Lloyd Powless, the tribe's medicine man, put a curse on the bank's upper management. He entered the main lobby holding the skin of a dead weasel aloft. Lloyd delivered an oath containing language like "Let your woman go barren and your children not prosper." Embarrassed and shocked, the First Wisconsin Trust reconsidered its role as a trustee for the Indians.

REFLECTIONS

Both stories highlight dramatic actions that went beyond the normal confrontation tactics. Each had a theatrical element as well a human side. Since the organizers had solid, long-term relationships with the local leaders, they trusted their advisors and were willing to take a risk in the action. You need to spend the time building a relationship before you can ask people to do something outside their comfort zone.

MINNEAPOLIS-SAINT PAUL, MINNESOTA

1976 to 1981
Twin Cities Organization (TCO)

★★★★

It was so cold the January that we moved to the Twin Cities, our plastic shower curtain shattered when we picked it up in the leased truck and all our liquor bottles exploded. The weather of "face freeze" winter days and humid, warm summers amid the lakes scattered around the metro area was part of what made living in the Twin Cities unforgettable.

My wife, Alana, and I had relocated so I could take over as the lead organizer of TCO. The group was a congregational-based citizens' organization with a mix of members from mainline Protestant and Catholic churches scattered around Minneapolis and Saint Paul. One of the major challenges was to identify an issue that united the congregations and moved them beyond their municipal boundaries. After a series of individual meetings with local leaders in which we heard stories about unscrupulous bank practices in certain neighborhoods, TCO took up the fight against redlining. Redlining is when companies refuse to offer home mortgages or home insurance to people in areas or neighborhoods deemed poor financial risks.

TCO asked the two largest financial institutions in the cities about releasing their records of mortgages in certain neighborhoods. Of course, the big banks refused. Surprisingly a couple of smaller financial institutions became allies with TCO and made it clear that they were willing to give mortgages to qualified, potential homeowners in those "bad" neighborhoods. Looking at the huge bank buildings outside the window of his downtown office, Walter Rasmussen, a progressive neighborhood banker, told me, "Some of those upper management finance guys think they have some authority, but I own the store." Rasmussen was a good friend of Sen. Walter Mondale and probably would have been appointed U.S. Treasury Secretary if Mondale had been elected president, but it isn't worth going down that road....

REFLECTIONS

During a series of meetings at St. Richard's Church in Richfield (a Minneapolis suburb), I met a young mother and homemaker named Mary Helgeson. I had an immediate sense of her talent. That encounter changed the direction of her life. She became involved in TCO and eventually emerged as a key leader. She enjoyed community organizing so much that she entered the field. She and her husband moved their young family to New York City so she could pursue her organizing career. They have been back in the Twin Cities for many years. Mary is the executive director of Hope Community, Inc., a strong community development organization. Hope, with more than 170 units of new and rehabbed housing, is changing the face of a much challenged neighborhood—one of the most diverse in the country. Mary and a strong, diverse staff engage hundreds of people each year in leadership, learning, community building, and organizing. You need to meet individually with people and get a sense of who they are and where they are in their lives. As you develop that relationship, look for potential talent and know there is a possibility that you could teach them something and that you, in turn, can learn something from them.

FORT WORTH, TEXAS

1981 to 1984
Allied Communities of Tarrant (ACT)

****

About 1,000 miles south of Minneapolis on Interstate 35 is one of the largest cowtowns in the United States. Fort Worth is proud of its cowboy history. It has redeveloped its stockyards and its downtown to reflect that heritage. The largest honky-tonk in the country, Billy Bob's, had just opened in the old stockyard area when Alana and I arrived.

Also, the Disciples of Christ denomination has a strong presence in Fort Worth. Texas Christian University and Brite Divinity School are Disciples of Christ institutions. In addition, there is a cultural district that features five museums, all well-endowed with oil wealth that is a source of civic pride.

I was the first staff person hired by the IAF Sponsoring Committee in Fort Worth. The committee was made up of clergy who wanted to create a congregation-based citizens' organization that would speak out and tackle social issues. My major task was to consolidate and add congregations to the existing committee so that it would be self-sustaining and have a large enough membership to be taken seriously. The goal was to create a tri-racial (Anglo, African-American and Hispanic) interfaith organization of at least 20 congregations.

The leaders I worked with the most were two

highly respected ministers, the Rev. Ed Wright of Ridglea Christian Church (Disciples of Christ) and the Rev. Nehemiah Davis of Mount Pisgah's Missionary Baptist Church. Rev. Davis helped me gain entry into the black churches. I had many individual meetings with pastors of the black churches and enjoyed access to a culture most whites never experience.

Rev. Wright was a leader who walked his talk more than any other person I'd ever met. He really believed that all people should be treated equally no matter their race, social status, or religion. I think his authenticity came from a sense of his own mortality. His grandfather and father died of kidney failure at relatively early ages.

In the process of building the congregation-based organization, we did what the IAF referred to as "actions," so as to develop esprit de corps among the leaders. One of the actions was to introduce ourselves and explain the organization's vision to Congressman Jim Wright, then Speaker of the U.S. House of Representatives. Rep. Wright was from Fort Worth and was one of the most powerful public officials in the country. A delegation of 12 clergy went to meet with him. After waiting half an hour and without anyone from his staff communicating what was going on, I raised the question of what we should say to Rep. Wright when he arrived. The clergy decided that if Rep. Wright arrived any later, they would ask him for an apology. It was agreed that Rev. Wright would have that assignment. Rep. Wright came in an hour late and greeted everyone warmly, but with no apology. When we formally started the meeting, Rev. Wright asked him to apologize to the group for his tardiness. I remember the speaker's eyes narrowing under his bushy eyebrows. I think Rep. Wright was inclined to give us a piece of his mind, but thought better of it and apologized to the pastors. Ultimately, though, he turned down an invitation to our founding convention, and we never had a working relationship with his local office while I was the lead organizer in Fort Worth.

We had the founding convention about two years after I arrived in Fort Worth. I had completed about 200 individual meetings with clergy to identify who among them saw their role as a pastor in the prophetic tradition. In other words, would they speak out and encourage members of their congregations to tackle societal issues that were affecting their lives.

I recommended to the leaders that we call the organization that we'd been building the Allied Communities of Tarrant (ACT). The rationale was that in the future we could go beyond the congregations for membership. Also, our churches were spread outside of Fort Worth into Tarrant County. Finally, the word "act" is defined as "the power to get something done." Over 20 congregations had joined ACT, paying dues of $500 to $20,000 dollars, depending on the size and budget of their institutions. ACT now had a budget with some "hard money" (that is, money raised by the organization internally) pledged. ACT went public with over 1,000 people attending from 20-plus congregations. At the founding convention, ACT asked Fort Worth Mayor Bob Bolen to sign an accountability pledge and agree to meet with ACT leaders to discuss issues of concern. Mayor Bolen agreed.

....

REFLECTIONS

The IAF teaches that there are two poles of power: organized money and organized people. In Fort Worth, I gained some understanding of what that meant. Also, I learned about the courage it takes to stand up for your values. My experience inside the black churches taught me about the power of the pulpit and the storied history of those institutions. ACT was taking a beginning step towards gaining recognition because it had a network of organized people through its congregations. However, Rev. Ed Wright lost his job because he was too outspoken on social issues for his middle-class church's conservative council. He took an assignment at a Dallas church, but he felt betrayed by some of his parishioners. About year and half after I left Fort Worth, Rev. Wright died from an unsuccessful kidney transplant. I was asked by his wife, Joyce, to eulogize him. It was great honor to speak before that packed church about Rev. Wright's legacy.

....

Through Ernie Cortez, my IAF supervisor in Fort Worth, I was introduced to Molly Ivins, who at that time was a regionally infamous Dallas Times Herald columnist. Molly and I became lifelong friends. Ernie was a longtime activist in Texas and, during the time I worked with him, he was awarded the MacArthur Fellows Foundation Award (sometimes called the "genius award") for his community organizing. Molly and Ernie were part of a network of progressives in Texas. I gained tremendous respect for leaders who acted on their beliefs, because in a state like Texas you can pay a high price for standing up for liberal values.

Molly went on to gain national recognition for her humorous and scathing books and columns. She warned her readers about electing Texas Gov. George W. Bush—the man she dubbed "Shrub"—to the presidency. At significant personal risk and sacrifice, Molly flew almost monthly to speak to ACLU chapters in small towns scattered around the United States. She had promised her friend, John Henry Faulk, a blacklisted radio announcer, on his death bed that she would do that in his memory. I learned that, obviously, another source of power is writing a nationally syndicated column that has a huge following. Someone said that Molly didn't have readers so much as a constituency. Many think that she'll be remembered as the Mark Twain of her generation.

Transition year of 1984

This was a year of significant change in Alana and my personal lives. We became parents at the age of 37. Our son, Ethan, was born on March 11 in Dallas, Texas. Besides becoming a father, I left the IAF network after 14 years. In a deliberate decision, Alana and I moved to

Denver instead of Seattle (our other choice), mostly for its better climate and geographic location. I had no firm job offers, but we felt I could find something before the IAF's three-month severance pay expired. Using my community organizing skills on a reconnaissance trip to Denver, I set up 25 individual meetings in five days to check out employment possibilities with local leaders before moving my family. I had one-on-one meetings with the likes of John Parr, president of the National Civic League; Ken Torp, chief of staff to Gov. Richard Lamm; and Rabbi Steve Foster, head of the largest Jewish congregation in Colorado. Alana had just finished her masters in urban affairs, earning straight A's at the University of Texas at Arlington and only had to complete her thesis. She planned to write it while staying home with Ethan.

I clearly remember putting on my straw Stetson and climbing into the front seat of the U-Haul truck. My wife's car with her two cats hiding under the seats was attached to the trailer hitch. We placed our infant son in his car seat between us in the cab and drove out of our quaint neighborhood of Mistletoe Heights, Texas, for the nearly 800-mile trip to Denver.

REFLECTIONS

When you're young, you tend to take more risks. The only people we knew in Colorado were my cousins, one living in Boulder and the other in Breckenridge.

Before we left Texas, I rented a house in the Platte Park neighborhood of Denver. I had been contemplating taking a union organizing job. What allowed this move to succeed was that I had a very supportive spouse. In my experience, when that is not the case a person's professional work suffers. My career path resonated with my wife's values, so she was encouraging when I reluctantly took a job offered by the Amalgamated Clothing and Textiles Workers Union. It was the only real offer I had. A stable and healthy personal life enhances your ability to pursue your professional goals.

So often we betray others

DENVER, COLORADO

1984 to Present

★ ★ ★ ★

When I look back at my 27-year career in Denver, it falls into three major areas: working in organized labor, working in the second administration of Mayor Federico Peña, and working with the Centers (now the Buechner Institute of Governance) at the School of Public Affairs at the University of Colorado Denver.

Amalgamated Clothing and Textiles Workers Union (ACTWU) December 1984 to June 1987

I wasn't naïve about the history or challenges facing the labor movement. I had been involved in projects with the United Auto Workers, American Federation of State, County and Municipal Employees and the United Mine Workers. I had become good friends with Ralph Helstein, the recently retired president of the Packing House Workers Union whom I met in Chicago through the IAF. Ralph had been close to Saul Alinsky. One of Saul's mentors was John L. Lewis, a giant in the labor movement. Saul wrote an unauthorized biography of Lewis. Also, I had grown up in anthracite coal country in northeastern Pennsylvania, a place with a tumultuous labor past. Even though my father regularly voted Republican, he was one of the doctors who regularly conducted a medical clinic sponsored by the International Ladies Garment Workers Union (ILGWU). My father once remarked that he admired the founding union leaders of ILGWU for their commitment to "cradle to grave" health care. With my encouragement, my younger sister became a UNISERV director in the Pennsylvania National Education Association many years after I left the labor movement.

Being a union organizer for ACTWU was the hardest job I ever had. Two years before I started working for ACTWU, President Reagan had fired all the striking federal air traffic controllers. The climate at the national level was hostile to unions. My two most memorable experiences at ACTWU were trying to organize at Carefree of Colorado, an awning manufacturing company in Broomfield, and preventing the AMF Head tennis racquet company in Boulder from moving overseas.

We had received a nervous phone call from Diane, an assembly line supervisor at Carefree of Colorado, about her interest in forming a union at the plant. Diane was a tough-looking, lanky, bleached-blond, tattooed, biker lady with a salt-of-the-earth personality. This popular shop leader was offended by the treatment of her fellow workers at the plant and by the substandard quality of the awning arm that Carefree was manufacturing.

It is incredibly hard to win a union election. We told Diane that she would be targeted by the company and that things would get rough for her. We mounted an organizing campaign, and the National Labor Relations Board (NLRB) authorized an election to be held. At that time Carefree was owned by the Scott Fetzer Company, a conglomerate based out of Cleveland, Ohio. It was a bitter election campaign with numerous allegations of NRLB violations, including illegal firings of pro-union workers. ACTWU won a Pyrrhic victory. The NLRB later ordered the company to reinstate 15 workers (three returned to work) and pay back pay of $168,379 for labor violations, but the organizing drive was decimated by the company's anti-union tactics. Managers at Scott Fetzer consciously decided that they would rather take the chance of violating labor law and risk closing the assembly plant in Broomfield than have it unionized.

Another battle concerned keeping the AMF Head tennis plant from leaving Colorado. Irwin Jacobs, an early corporate raider based out of Minneapolis, engineered a hostile takeover of AMF Head. Soon after Jacobs acquired the company, the employees were notified that the assembly plant would be relocated to Austria. Using my community organizing background, I identified some sympathetic Boulder clergy and approached Congressman Tim Wirth and State Representative David Skaggs, both from Boulder, seeking their support. Finally, I used a former labor contact from Minneapolis. I called David Roe, the president of the Minnesota AFL-CIO, and told him the story. On a snowy winter night, we held an emotional meeting for the AMF Head workers in a packed church basement in Boulder. Wirth, Skaggs, and Eldon Cooper, president of the Colorado AFL-CIO, rallied the crowd. I remember a rousing chorus of "Solidarity Forever" being sung. The behind-the-scenes leverage worked. We delayed the plant moving overseas for more than two years.

REFLECTIONS

A fundamental right in a democratic society is for workers in both the public and private sectors to be free to organize. I can't predict the future of unions, but a workforce that is 11.3 percent organized still needs to be taken seriously. Saul used to say that if only 10 percent of any population is organized, it is still a powerful presence. When I contemplate what lies ahead for this country, I think of a quote from Frederick Douglass that we have hanging in our living room: "Those who profess to favor freedom and yet deprecate agitation are people who want crops without plowing the ground; they want rain without thunder and lightning; they want the ocean without the roar of its many waters. The struggle may be a moral one, or it may be a physical one, or it may be both. But it must be a struggle. Power concedes nothing without a demand; it never has and it never will."

Second Mayoral Campaign of Federico Peña
Spring 1987

The ACTWU director in Chicago, Arthur Lovey, whose jurisdiction covered Colorado locals, graciously granted me a paid leave of absence to work on Federico Peña's second mayoral campaign. One of the reasons Art sanctioned this was because Peña's victory was important to the broader labor movement. The economy in Denver in the late 1980s was grim. The hope was that the proposed new airport was going to generate many new construction jobs. Organized labor wanted a sympathetic mayor in office. John Parr recommended me to Peña's campaign staff, and I dove into the intense reelection operation. With my contacts in organized labor, naturally my focus was that constituency. Convincing union leaders that Peña was a better choice than his opponent, Don Bain, wasn't the major challenge; it was getting the rank and file excited about his second term. At one point in the reelection campaign, our poll numbers had us down by a huge margin. I planned a meeting for organized labor at the campaign headquarters to try to regain momentum. We jammed well over 100 union activists into a room. I remember telling the mayor to take off his sport coat, loosen his tie, and roll up his shirtsleeves and fire up the crowd. Mayor Peña was always underestimated as a speaker. He gave a rousing speech and excited the rank-and-file leaders. Many of them volunteered to do the grunt work that is critical to every successful campaign. Peña won, and the unions rightfully claimed credit for the critical role they played in helping him achieve a victory. I had never been promised a job in the second administration, but I demonstrated skills that built my credibility. I had a couple of job offers and consulted with friends about the opportunities. I left ACTWU on good terms and took a job at the New Airport Office.

REFLECTIONS

When self-interest and a plan for a better future converge in politics, it is a powerful force. Peña's vision to "imagine a great city" tied to a new airport that would create a lot of jobs energized many people from organized labor, especially construction workers. The Peña campaign harnessed that excitement and focused it.

New Airport Office
Summer 1987 to winter 1988

The charge to the New Airport Office was to write the Environmental Impact Statement required by the Environmental Protection Agency. The New Airport Office also was created to provide the public with information and make presentations on the project.

My real work was much more political, however. The annexation of land in Adams County for the new airport had to be approved by Denver voters. Even though the public knew that Stapleton Airport was outdated, they regarded its convenient location as a huge positive. The 25-to-30-mile drive to the new airport was seen by the average citizen as a major negative. Conversely, the overwhelming majority of the community around Park Hill wanted Stapleton moved. I used my background as a community organizer and began meeting one-on-one with the pastors from the neighborhoods around Stapleton.

In those individual meetings I heard concerns around the issues of safety and noise. Most of the clergy felt it was just a matter of time before a plane crashed, and families living near Stapleton would pay dearly when that tragedy occurred. At times the noise from the planes taking off and landing was intolerable. Many members of their congregations had complained. Several of the pastors expressed anger at having a Sunday sermon ruined because the weather had changed and planes were flying over their churches to land at a runway designated by the air traffic controllers. In meeting with the clergy I also stumbled across an additional piece of information. Some of the regional judicatory heads of their denominations were frustrated with Stapleton. Several of the bishops presided over huge territories and frequently, when clergy and lay leaders were flying to Denver for meetings, flights would be canceled because planes couldn't land during rough weather due to the inadequate runways. The bishops had to cancel those meetings, costing them time and money.

The clergy drafted and signed a letter of support for the new airport. We even got a couple bishops to write their own letters of support. Ten clergy held a press conference to announce their support for the new airport. A leader of the opposition was quoted as saying "they even got G-d on their side."

After the Denver voters approved the annexation for the new airport, another obstacle threatened the project. Opponents argued that Adams County voters should be allowed to approve the land deal as well, so they petitioned and won the right to hold a second election. Adams County has a large blue-collar population, and at that time many areas were still rural. Once again I tapped into my community organizing skills and created a committee called Construction Says Yes. The members were both union and non-union leaders connected with the construction industry. An old ally from organized labor, Bob Ozinga, organizer for the Building and Construction Trade Council, was a key member of the committee. Many construction workers lived in Adams County, and a large turnout from that constituency was critical. The new airport would be one of the largest public works projects in the United States. Colorado's economy was suffering from a recent oil bust. I remember agitating those construction industry leaders on the committee about how important it was to communicate to their workers the consequences of losing the election. The Construction Says Yes committee held a rally to motivate its members. The turnout surprised everyone.

Over 1,000 construction workers and their families streamed into a meeting hall in the heart of Adams County. Roused by speakers, including Mayor Peña, several in the audience committed to work the phones and walk precincts. The construction workers were essential to the victory in Adams County.

REFLECTIONS

The old adage that a community organizer's most important organ is his ears was once again proven correct. I took the time to meet with the neighborhood clergy and listen to their concerns before I assumed anything. As I was muddling along, I discovered that a powerful ally existed in the denominations' judicatory heads for reasons others hadn't known. Getting into the field and meeting one-on-one with leaders is fundamental to understanding and successfully tackling any issue. Another lesson is that when given a clear goal and properly challenged to produce, a group of connected leaders from organizations and businesses can turn out large numbers of people. Those construction leaders had the networks and relationships to produce the huge turnout, and they had the organizational structure to follow up with those who attended the dramatic event.

*Mayor's Office: Administrative Assistant
to Federico Peña
January 1989 to May 1991*

After the victory in Adams County, the New Airport Office was folded into regular airport operations. The engineers and architects took over from the "politicos," since our work was done. I now had time on my hands. An idea that intrigued me was creating an education, recreation, and child-care facility for travelers with young children. I had seen versions of this concept at a couple of other airports. Martha Daley at the Mayor's Office on Childcare and Alby Segall at the Children's Museum were willing partners, and we gathered support for the project. Ironically, since Stapleton was going to close in a few years, airport management there seemed open to new ideas. I helped raise over $100,000 from airport-connected vendors. We opened Kidsport, which weary parents with small children deeply appreciated, as a place for education and play. Sadly, it was not carried over to Denver International Airport. Partly this was because it didn't fit in with the big, new airport image and because of post 9/11 security concerns.

Shortly after Kidsport opened, I was invited to join the mayor's staff by Katherine Archuleta, one of Peña's most trusted aides. I was to handle all of the mayor's appointments to the myriad boards and commissions that existed in Denver. At that time there were approximately 100 boards and commissions with about 500 members. Several of these boards, such as the Board of Ethics, Denver Urban Renewal Authority, Civil Service Commission, Board of Water Commissioners, Denver Housing Authority, and the Winter Park Association Board, to name a few, had significant power. Also as part of that job, I staffed the mayor on his appointments to the Denver County Court. Peña welcomed input, and each time a court appointment came up, I received calls—usually from well-connected attorneys—who were lobbying for a friend or colleague. Sometimes that also happened when other powerful boards had openings.

The other major area of responsibility I held was as liaison to organized labor. Mayor Peña felt the need to have a person in his office designated to deal with issues that labor deemed important. Because of my background, I had some credibility with labor leaders. However, it usually was a thankless job since we almost never could give labor leaders everything they wanted.

Finally, there was the ubiquitous "duties as assigned." On occasion I acted as a liaison between the Mayor's Office and the Planning Department dealing with a neighborhood issue. Lisa Carlson and Ken Torp from the Centers at the University of Colorado Denver were the facilitators for the planning process involving City Park. I had been through the Denver Community Leadership Forum in 1989, so I had some knowledge about the process of reaching agreement through building consensus. I was representing the Mayor's Office as a stakeholder in a group that was to develop a recommendation to the mayor and the council on expanding into City Park land for a larger park headquarters and new roads. Ken and Lisa were the facilitators for the process, which ultimately was thwarted when politically connected attorneys from the nearby neighborhood of Park Hill sued the city to prevent the expansion and won.

Peña decided not to run for a third term, even though most pundits thought he would have won handily. The mayor's staff was offered help through an outside job counselor to explore other employment opportunities. I stayed until Mayor Peña left office.

REFLECTIONS

It was exciting working for Mayor Peña, even though there were challenges in being part of an administration that was sometimes unfairly attacked, had its own internal power struggles, and at times made mistakes. The power of elected officials and their staffs comes purely from the position. You bask in the glow of being an aide to a powerful public official. However, you must realize that kind of power is ephemeral. Once your patron is defeated or decides not to run for reelection, the power vanishes. You need a strong ego, friends, and family support systems to navigate that loss.

Another Transition Period
May 1991 to May 1992

I had worked continuously since I graduated from college. Now I decided to take a stretch off before I began looking for another job in earnest. I focused on three goals: to travel overseas, run a local marathon, and improve my typing skills.

The family joke has been that my mother-in-law was coming for a two-week visit that summer so it would be a good time for me to head overseas. I hadn't traveled alone abroad for over 20 years. My wife called the trip my "walkabout." A major criterion for the country I would tour was that it had to be inexpensive. One day while jogging with Ken Torp, we were discussing my travel plans and he said that a friend of his had just returned from Czechoslovakia. The friend said that his expenses were very reasonable. I had never been to Eastern Europe and the Velvet Revolution had just occurred there the year before, so I decided I would make the journey.

It is important for me to learn as much as possible about a country before I arrive, so I purchased numerous Czech guide books and maps at Denver's famous Tattered Cover bookstore. I'd listen to audio books or buy a book by a Czech author. I watched movies made in Czechoslovakia and met with people who had visited the country or lived there. It was part of my adult education.

Almost 20 years later I still remember the burgeoning culture and arts of Prague, the ancient Jewish cemetery where people were buried in layers, the painting and graffiti of the revolution that were on a wall that went on for hundreds of yards, and a trip to a historic hot springs spa that was very different from the ones in Colorado. However, my strongest memory was walking through a concentration camp called Terezin. It is sometimes referred as the children's concentration camp because 15,000 children under the age of 15 passed through its gates and less than one percent survived. Terezin is the kind of place that touches you at a very deep level.

I had run for years, but never entered a marathon. I did it for several reasons. Running always has been a stress reducer; I had had to manage my time each day to schedule training runs; and it was a way to maintain my weight and still be able eat mostly what I wanted. The discipline of training and running 26.2 miles reinforces the knowledge that other goals are obtainable if you set your mind to it. I completed the Fifth Hellenic Cup marathon sponsored by a local Greek organization. At the finish line, I was cheered on by my wife and eight-year-old son. The Hellenic Cup race was discontinued a couple years after I ran it.

I never had taken a formal typing class. I was not very good on a keyboard. I usually had secretaries who typed for me and I went to a college where professors would accept handwritten papers. However, I knew I had to retool as the computer was making horizontal organizations the norm. I enrolled at the Emily Griffith Opportunity School, along with other older adults looking to acquire new skills in the changing marketplace. I took a typing class not once but twice, and it has proven to be an invaluable skill.

The economy in Denver in 1992 was not good. I spent about nine months looking hard for jobs and got close to being hired on a couple of occasions. It was a humbling experience, but I learned from it.

REFLECTIONS

If you're between jobs and can take advantage of the situation, I recommend you travel for the adventure and to open your mind to new cultures; engage in disciplined exercise for reducing stress and making your body stronger; and take a class to learn or improve a skill.

Public Facilitator with the Center for Public-Private Cooperation and the Center for the Improvement of Public Management at the School of Public Affairs at the University of Colorado Denver

May 1992 to May 2011

I was hired to facilitate community projects at "the Centers" in May 1992 and received a full-time appointment in November 1992. The director of the Centers, Ken Torp, and my long-time colleague, Lisa

Carlson, joked that they had to hire me because I kept hanging around. After joining the Centers staff, I was frequently asked if it was difficult to become a facilitator with my background in politics and community organizing. Early on at the Centers, I even did a training session on the similarities and differences between the role of a community organizer and a facilitator.

What made the transition from community and political organizer to facilitator relatively easy is that a central role in each profession is that of an advocate, a value and strength of mine throughout my career. A facilitator is an advocate for the *process* not a specific issue—ensuring that every voice has a seat at the table; promoting a planning process that is open and transparent; enabling everyone to participate as an equal; and striving for consensus-based decision-making.

In cleaning out my office upon my retirement in 2011, I saw files reminding me of particular clients I had over the almost two decades I was with the Centers. I estimate that I had at least 80 clients scattered around the state, including six initiatives launched by The Colorado Trust. The Colorado Trust is one of the largest foundations in the State of Colorado. Its mission is "advancing the health and well-being of the people of Colorado," which is reflected in the diverse initiatives I worked on. They included Teen Pregnancy Prevention, Supporting Immigrant and Refugee Families, Suicide Prevention, the Partnership in Health and Violence Prevention. What was unique about The Trust was that instead of imposing a rigid program model, it funded community-based planning processes to develop local solutions. Using selection criteria such as community readiness, future sustainability, and support from other local organizations, projects were funded for a minimum of three years.

Through this work I discovered that it's irrelevant whether projects are located in cities, suburbs, small towns, rural areas, or resort communities. You must be open to working with all kinds of people and all types of organizations. You must be stimulated by the idiosyncrasies of these locales. You need to be excited about the possibility of learning about different cultures. You must let go of stereotypes and approach the experience with a conscious open-mindedness. You achieve satisfaction from identifying potential grass-roots leaders and mentoring them. It is essential that people who want to do this work relish getting out of their comfort zones and jumping into the unfamiliar.

I enjoyed my years as a facilitator/project consultant and on several occasions the local stakeholders group gave me a plaque or a gift of appreciation, which have long been the source of good-natured ribbing from my colleagues!

I believe my community and political organizing experience translated into making me a very good field facilitator. I have a clear understanding of how and why it's important to build relationships with leaders from the local community. Because of my background, I am committed to getting out and moving around the community so I can better understand it, especially in the rural areas. Because of my own efforts trying to organize change in communities, I'm aware of the challenges locals face. Also, I learned a long time ago about both self-interest and enlightened self-interest and what motivates people to get involved. Self-interest is your own personal interest and enlightened self-interest is a concern for the welfare of the broader community. The variety of clients and the different areas I've worked in around Colorado have given me a deep appreciation for the dedication and talent that exist among grassroots leaders.

A Mark Twain quote came to mind as I traveled to these distinct communities around Colorado. "Travel is fatal to prejudice, bigotry, and narrow-mindedness, and many of our people need it sorely on these accounts. Broad, wholesome, charitable views of men and things cannot be acquired by vegetating in one little corner of the earth all one's life."

While at the Centers, I also had many clients in the government sector. I cite three examples of successful collaborative efforts and the factors that led to that success:

- Passing a child car seat safety law in the mid-1990s required *having the right people at the table*. The Colorado Department of Transportation was the lead agency that brought together a diverse group of pediatricians, emergency room personnel, children's advocates, representatives from organizations that focus on traffic safety, and nonprofits such as the American Automobile Association and Mothers Against Drunk Driving. After a series of facilitated meetings, researching the issue of car seat safety, and hearing presentations from experts, the group crafted legislation that ultimately became law. In 1995, the state mandated that children under age 16 be required to use seatbelts or car seats in the front and back seats. The credibility and organizational clout of the stakeholders enabled the passage of this legislation. To realize that in my role as the facilitator for the group I played a part in preventing children from getting seriously injured or killed in car crashes is very gratifying.

- Developing a skateboarding park for a Denver city councilwoman taught me to *never underestimate or stereotype your stakeholders*. In the late 1990s, skateboarders were frowned upon by the general public. Punk-looking, strangely-garbed, wild-haired youngsters racing by pedestrians on city streets or sliding on building handrails were a common encounter. Councilwoman Joyce Foster decided to form the Skateboarders Task Force and I agreed to be the facilitator, aware of my own biases against the "boarders." The young people on the task force quickly dispelled my prejudices. A bright orange-haired young woman with a stud in her face became one of the leaders of the group. The task force made site visits to identify possible skateboarding park locations, researched the few other skateboarding parks that had been built in the country, worked on design layout, and made public presentations—including one to then-Mayor Wellington Webb. The stakeholders finished their recommendations and waited and waited while Councilwoman Foster and her allies kept moving the process forward inside the city. In 2003, the Denver Skatepark was dedicated. The following year an article appeared in the respected alternative newspaper, *Westword*, quoting a spokeswoman for the Parks and Recreation Department who said the park "has been a raging success." I enjoyed this project because it is a concrete reminder, in more ways than one, that good recommendations from a task force with strong internal champions have a chance to become reality.

- School revitalization for Denver Public Schools succeeded because of *a good outreach strategy combined with community readiness*. I was contacted by the Southeast Area Superintendent to facilitate a planning process to revitalize three schools: Bradley Elementary, Montclair Elementary, and Hill Middle School. The goals were to increase enrollment particularly from the surrounding neighborhoods and to strengthen academic achievement. Working with the principal in each school, we set up stakeholder groups that included the principal, administrators, teachers, office staff, parents of students and, when possible, representatives from the nearby neighborhood associations. In the selection of the teachers, I made an effort to find out which ones were active in the union. From my experience, respected teachers who were involved in the union usually had strong networks inside the buildings and potentially had the resources from the Denver Classroom Teachers' Association behind them. Each of the schools approached the goals in its own way. The most successful effort was at Montclair. The new and energetic principal, Shannon Hagerman, as well as members of the stakeholders group went door-to-door handing out information to the residents about the school. The school hosted a community rally at my suggestion and I trained members of the group on how to conduct the meeting. The event was a big success and John Temple, a neighborhood resident and then-publisher of the *Rocky Mountain News*, attended. He wrote an excellent story that appeared prominently in the paper about what Montclair was attempting to do and the palpable excitement generated at the community meeting. The article was a turning point, and Montclair started to rebuild its reputation as a successful neighborhood school.

REFLECTIONS

Magic can happen with stakeholder groups that have real power to come up with answers. Stakeholders in public life must be clear about their charge, have good leadership, value collaboration, be willing to listen to different perspectives, be committed to doing their homework, follow up on assignments, and reach decisions based upon consensus. A good public facilitator has to be disinterested in the final outcome, that is, he or she must be willing to let others make the decisions at their own pace and based on their own self-interest.

Theater Producer
March 2010 to November 2012

By a strange coincidence, I was invited to the premiere of the play, *Red Hot Patriot: The Kick-Ass Wit of Molly Ivins* in Philadelphia in 2010. It all started a few months earlier when I arranged for Sanford Horwitt to speak at an event that I had organized sponsored jointly by University of Colorado Denver and the University of Denver in celebration of the 100th anniversary of Saul Alinsky's birth. Sandy was an old acquaintance from my days at the IAF in Chicago. When I first met him, he was writing a book on Saul's life. His book, *Let Them Call Me Rebel, Saul Alinsky His Life and Legacy*, has become one of the seminal works on Alinsky's life.

In a casual conversation with Sandy, I had mentioned my friendship with Molly. By a quirk of fate, it turns out that Sandy's twin sisters-in-law had just written a play on Molly's life. Two-time Golden Globe Award winner and Academy Award and Tony Award nominee Kathleen Turner had agreed to portray Molly. Sandy offered to get tickets for Alana and me when the play opened.

On March 19, 2010, we saw Turner capture Molly's essence with the Philadelphia Theater Company. I immediately told Alana I wanted to bring the show to Denver. Little did I realize how challenging it would be to bring that goal to fruition. It took two and a half years before I found someone willing to mount the play. During that period, I built a support team of colleagues and friends who were helpful in strategizing and encouraged me to continue the quest. In moving around the Denver theater community, I met with nine directors—all of whom turned me down for myriad reasons. Then I was referred to Brian Freeland, the dynamic and respected founder of the LIDA Project, a small experimental black-box theater company. Brian was the only one willing to take the risk, and he pulled together the crew that would create the play. The irony was that once I finally had the production team, it took me only two and a half *weeks* to raise the $10,000 necessary to produce it! Because I understand turn out and working with the media, we received very good coverage of the play. Alana and I, using our own considerable networks, contacted many friends and former colleagues to help spread the word. Finally, we timed the opening to occur at the height of the political season. We opened it right before the November 2012 election. The play was a hit, with nearly all performances sold out. Our production of *Red Hot Patriot* received the award for Best Political Theater of the year from the alternative newspaper and website *Westword*.

REFLECTIONS

My organizing, political, and facilitator background taught me to accept rejection and not take it personally. My experience allowed me keep going in an entirely new venue. I believed that some director out there would be willing to make this happen and that I would find that person. Also, I was not afraid to make the ask to raise the funds needed. Bottom line is that building grassroots organizations is good preparation for doing almost anything in public life.

CLOSING THOUGHTS

★★★★

I grew up in the small rural town of Noxen, Pennsylvania, where my father started his medical practice and where we lived until I was 12 years old. Noxen had a population of about 500 people who lived in the "back mountains" of northern Appalachia. Later this rural community became well known for hosting the annual Rattlesnake Round-Up festival, where a prize was given to the person who caught the largest rattlesnake in the rugged hills. I went to an old wooden schoolhouse where three grades occupied the same classroom. My schoolmates were children of tannery workers, hard-scrabble farmers, and blue-collar families eking out a living in the area. I was too young to understand, but some of my fellow students were dirt poor. We were the only Jewish children in the community and among the few who enjoyed a comfortable middle-class lifestyle.

Among my family members and friends are many doctors, lawyers, psychologists, and professionals in traditional occupations. My career often has been hard for some of them to understand. My Aunt Gracie asked what I "did for a living" every time she saw me. I would explain each time, but I knew she never understood my work. I am convinced that Aunt Gracie thought I was an undercover agent for the CIA! I always thought this was humorous, but I appreciate the difficulty people had understanding my career, given my middle-class background. In many ways, though, my career was a natural outcome of my early experiences. Growing up in Noxen and experiencing the idealism of the 1960s significantly shaped my world view. As a result, I empathize with people who are considered underdogs or the "others" in our society.

Since my retirement party in June of 2011, hosted by the School of Public Affairs, Alana and I have begun thinking about the future. Alana, who also has led an active public life, retired a year and half before I did to manage her mother's Alzheimer's treatment and personal affairs.

There is a certain irony that—as we close this phase of our careers and discuss how to use our talents and wisdom in new ways—our son, Ethan, is working hard to launch his. It seems only fair that people of my generation who can afford to retire should get out of the way and make room for Ethan's generation.

After being together for over four decades and blessed with good health in our sixties, Alana and I are committed to maintaining our zest for life's journey as this new chapter unfolds. In the years ahead, I hope to have many more meaningful experiences that will provide fresh stories to write about and translate into new life lessons.

ACKNOWLEDGMENTS

★★★★

I would like to thank my colleague and friend Lisa Carlson, who came up with the idea of a white paper on my 45-year career even though when I first heard her suggestion I wasn't very enthusiastic about it. Lisa is a superb and experienced facilitator who was always willing to share her knowledge and insights on any of my challenging projects

I want to recognize Dean Paul Teske of the School of Public Affairs, who generously agreed to pay me to write the white paper. I am sure without that incentive it would have been an unfinished task. Also, thanks to my colleague and friend Diane Carman, whose excellent skills I admired when she wrote a weekly column at the Denver *Post* and who helped me shape this book and make it better.

Other people whom I've respected or been influenced by or who supported my career include the following:

Community organizing: Fred Ficken, a VISTA buddy who became a large property manager and decent, successful businessman; Peter Martinez, my friend and mentor from the IAF; Greg Pierce, one of my oldest friends since we met at the IAF in 1970 who is now a successful entrepreneur, book publisher, and community leader; and Mike Gecan, one of the most talented and effective IAF organizers in the country.

Politics: Mayor Federico Peña handled Denver's

day-to-day management and at the same time had the vision to lead a city; Deborah Senn, an old friend from the McGovern campaign who demonstrated courageous leadership as the populist Insurance Commissioner of the State of Washington; and former Colorado First Lady Jeannie Ritter, who against her advisers' counsel met with and supported grassroots leaders working on suicide prevention all across Colorado.

Organized labor: Richard Bensinger, who recruited me into ACTWU, a dedicated and intense labor organizer who isn't afraid to criticize the unions while being committed to their values; Mike Bello, an NLRB attorney, who tenaciously pursued the Scott Fetzer Company for its illegal actions against the workers at Carefree; and Jon Wilderman, a workers compensation attorney, who was the consummate professional when we monitored the Teamster elections together.

Facilitation/project consultant: Ken Torp, a man of many talents and interests who was willing to strategize about my projects and reflect on larger world issues on our runs together. Tom McCoy, a colleague of charm and wisdom who recently died and was one of the people who always encouraged me to write about my experiences.

Family: My wife, Alana, and son, Ethan, who have always been supportive of my career paths; my siblings, who are involved with making human lives better whether it is as an oncologist (brother Bruce), teachers union representative (sister Sheila), or grief counselor (sister Carol). These values around service stem from our mother, Bertha, who battled multiple sclerosis for over 30 years yet remained a kind and loving person, and our father, Lester, who was a dedicated and highly-respected country doctor.